D1544664

CARS
on the Move

Willow Clark

PowerKiDS press

New York

For Dan, and the thrilling twisty road ahead

Published in 2010 by The Rosen Publishing Group, Inc.
29 East 21st Street, New York, NY 10010

First Edition

Editor: Nicole Pristash
Book Design: Kate Laczynski
Photo Researcher: Jessica Gerweck

Photo Credits: Cover, p. 1 Mark Scott/Getty Images; p. 4 Car Culture/Getty Images; p. 6 Time Life Pictures/Getty Images; p. 8 © www.istockphoto.com/Joe_Potato; p. 10 © Courtesy of Shelby SuperCars; pp. 12, 18, 20 Shutterstock.com; pp. 14–15 Simon Bruty/Getty Images; p. 16 Jonathan Daniel/Getty Images.

Library of Congress Cataloging-in-Publication Data

Clark, Willow.
  Cars on the move / Willow Clark. — 1st ed.
      p. cm. — (Transportation station)
  Includes index.
  ISBN 978-1-4358-9333-7 (library binding) — ISBN 978-1-4358-9754-0 (pbk.) — ISBN 978-1-4358-9755-7 (6-pack)
  1. Automobiles—Juvenile literature. I. Title.
  TL206.C58 2010
  629.222—dc22
                                        2009023767

Manufactured in the United States of America

CPSIA Compliance Information: Batch #WW10PK: For Further Information contact Rosen Publishing, New York, New York at 1-800-237-9932

Contents

This car is a 1969 Pontiac GTO. Some believe that this car was the first true muscle car.

Let's Hit the Road!

We see cars everywhere! They are a big part of our lives. We use cars to get around town and to take trips.

All cars are not used only to get from place to place, though. Many cars, such as stock cars, are made to go super fast. Other cars are built with powerful engines and are made to look cool. These special cars are called hot rods and muscle cars.

This book will talk more about all these amazing machines and show you what the car of tomorrow might be like. Fasten your seat belts and get ready to learn all about cars!

This picture shows a 1912 Ford Model T taxi in Great Britain. The Ford Model T was the first car to be produced in many countries at the same time.

Going Horseless

Before there were cars, people used horse-drawn **carriages** to get around. Then, the 1880s saw the invention of the gas-powered engine and the gas-powered car. By 1910, dozens of companies were making cars in the United States and around the world.

Cars have changed a lot since then. Today's cars have many **features**, such as soft seats, seat belts, and windshield wipers, that make the cars safe and comfortable. Today's cars go much faster, too. The 1908 Ford Model T had a top speed of around 40 miles per hour (64 km/h). That is slower than today's highway speeds!

Here you can see what a car's engine looks like. Many parts inside the engine work together to power the car.

How Cars Work

Have you ever wondered how a car works? Cars are powered by an engine. Inside an engine, gas from a gas tank mixes with air and turns into **vapor**. Parts called spark plugs cause the vapor to burn, which forces parts inside the engine to move. This movement is used to power the car.

The outside of a car, called the body, needs to be strong to keep the people riding inside of it safe. The bodies of today's cars are made mostly out of steel, which is very strong. Other parts of the body may be made of lighter **materials**, such as **aluminum**, **fiberglass**, or plastics.

The Ultimate Aero sports car, shown here, has butterfly doors. Butterfly doors not only move out, but they move up as well.

Cars Large and Small

Passenger cars are cars that people ride in every day. There are many kinds of passenger cars. Compact cars are small cars. SUVs, or sport-utility vehicles, are large cars that have the seating space of cars but can be used like trucks.

Sports cars are another type of passenger car. Sports cars are fast. They sit low to the ground and are often painted with bright colors. Sports cars have **aerodynamic** shapes, which helps them go fast. The fastest widely produced sports car is the Shelby SuperCars Ultimate Aero. It has reached a speed of 257 miles per hour (414 km/h)!

Flames, such as the ones on this hot rod, are some of the most popular things hot-rod owners have painted on their cars. Pages 14–15: A Formula One race car.

Hot Rods and Muscle Cars

Hot rods and muscle cars are cars that people collect. Hot rods are cars that have been rebuilt for speed. Some hot rods are small cars that have a bigger car's engine in them. Others are old cars that have had newer engines put in. Hot rods are known for their wild paint jobs.

Muscle cars are known for their big, powerful engines. Muscle cars are American-made cars that were built mostly in the 1960s and 1970s. They were often used in drag races, which are types of street races. The Pontiac GTO and the Chevrolet Chevelle are common types of muscle cars.

INFORMATION STATION

1 In 1899, Jacob German became the first person to be arrested for speeding. He was driving 12 miles per hour (19 km/h)!

2 William Taft, the twenty-seventh president of the United States, was the first president to own a car.

3 NASCAR drivers generally race at speeds between 175 and 200 miles per hour (282–322 km/h).

4 In 1916, 55 percent of the cars in the world were Ford Model Ts.

5 More than one million Toyota and Lexus **hybrid cars** have been sold around the world.

6 The first three-color stoplight was invented by a police officer, William Potts, in Detroit, Michigan, in 1920.

7 It is believed that by 2011, there will be nearly a billion cars on the roads throughout the world.

This picture shows a NASCAR race in Brooklyn, Michigan. NASCAR races are the most popular type of stock-car races in the world.

Built for Speed

Many cars are made to look good, but some cars, such as race cars, are made for speed. One type of race car is a stock car. A stock car is a race car that has a body that looks like a passenger car. However, the rest of a stock car, especially its engine, is built for racing.

Dodge Chargers are often used as stock cars. A Dodge Charger passenger car has a top speed of around 145 miles per hour (233 km/h). However, a Dodge Charger stock car hit a top speed of 244.9 miles per hour (394 km/h) in 2007. This broke the stock car world speed record.

A Formula One car has a wing on its front and on its back end. Wings help hold the car close to the ground. This helps the car go faster.

Formula One

A Formula One race car is a race car built by teams, and it is raced in track races. The body of a Formula One race car is long and thin, and the car sits low to the ground.

Formula One racing began in 1950 with 7 races. Today, there are 17 to 19 races held around the world each season.

Formula One race cars are some of the fastest cars in the world. In 2006, Alan van der Merwe pushed his Honda Formula One car to 220.57 miles per hour (354.97 km/h) at Bonneville Salt Flats, in Utah. This set the speed record for a Formula One car!

This is a Toyota Prius hybrid car. The Prius is one of the best-selling hybrid cars in the world.

Going Green

When cars burn gas, they let out **exhaust**, which is bad for the air. People have many ideas about how to make cars more **fuel efficient**. Fuel-efficient cars work like other cars, but they use less gas. Cars that use less gas are green, which means they are better for the **environment**.

Today, several types of green cars are available. **Hybrid cars**, such as the Toyota Prius, use less gas. There are also fully electric cars and cars that run on **biofuels**. Carmakers are working toward making cars even more efficient. Cars of tomorrow will be even greener than today's cars are.

Cars in Our World

To some people, cars are just a means of traveling. To others, cars are much more. Collectors see muscle cars and hot rods as works of art because of their wild paint jobs and rebuilt engines. Race fans enjoy watching race cars as they speed around tracks and break records.

Cars have helped make our lives both easier and more exciting. Today, people are working to make them better for the environment. This way, cars will not only be some of the most useful and interesting vehicles in the world, they will also be safer for our world!

Glossary

aerodynamic (er-oh-dy-NA-mik) Made to move through the air easily.

aluminum (uh-LOO-muh-num) A type of metal.

biofuels (by-oh-FYOO-elz) Things made out of natural, raw materials that are used to make power.

carriages (KAR-ij-ez) Wheeled objects used to carry people or things.

environment (en-VY-ern-ment) All the living things and conditions of a place.

exhaust (ig-ZOST) Smoky air made by burning gas.

features (FEE-churz) Special parts.

fiberglass (FY-ber-glas) A material made of glass and other things.

fuel efficient (FYOO-el ih-FIH-shent) Operable using little fuel.

hybrid cars (HY-brud KAHRZ) Cars that have an engine that runs on gasoline and a motor that runs on electricity.

materials (muh-TEER-ee-ulz) What something is made of.

passenger (PA-sin-jur) A person who rides in or on a moving thing.

vapor (VAY-per) A liquid that has turned into a gas.

Index

A
air, 9, 21
aluminum, 9

B
biofuels, 21

C
carriages, 7
companies, 7

E
engine(s), 5, 7, 9, 13,
  17, 22
environment, 21–22
exhaust, 21

F
features, 7
fiberglass, 9
Ford Model T(s), 7, 15

G
gas, 9, 21

H
hot rods, 5, 13, 22

I
invention, 7

M
materials, 9

P
part(s), 5, 9

S
seat belts, 5, 7
seats, 7
shapes, 11
spark plugs, 9
speed(s), 7, 11, 13–14, 17

U
United States, 7, 14

V
vapor, 9

Web Sites

Due to the changing nature of Internet links, PowerKids Press has developed an online list of Web sites related to the subject of this book. This site is updated regularly. Please use this link to access the list: www.powerkidslinks.com/stat/car/